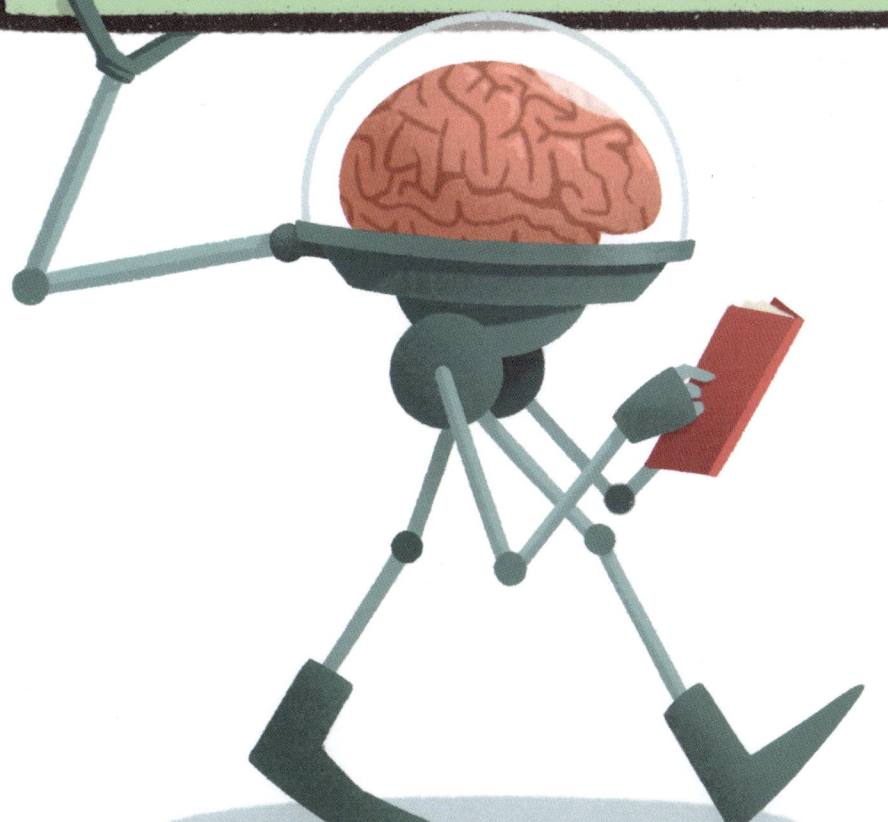

Dedicated to young people
in the North of England
who inspired this story

First Published 2023
Independently published

Text copyright © 2023 Natalie Morrell & Josh Hawkins
Illustrations copyright © 2023 Mark Bird

All rights reserved. No part of this publication may be reproduced, distributed, or transmitted in any form or by any means, including photocopying, recording, or other electronic or mechanical methods, without the prior written permission of the publisher.

Book design by Mark Bird

ISBN: 9798862766721

www.theknottedproject.co.uk
www.hawkdancetheatre.com

With thanks to our partners and funders: Supported using public funding by Arts Council England, Blaize Rural Touring Schemes, Children and Young People's Dance Network North, The Grand Theatre Blackpool and Northern School of Contemporary Dance

THE GREATEST ROBOT EVER

Written by The Knotted Project & Hawk Dance Theatre

Illustrated by Mark Bird

A world of junk piled high like mountains,
Where sparks explode into firework fountains.

Twisted metal at skyscraper heights,
Technology buzzing with shimmering lights.

Piles of scrap for jumping and sliding,
A playground of fun where robots are hiding!

You might just find them, if you look hard,
Welcome to the famous Robot Junk Yard...

There are robots everywhere, each shape and size.
There are robots everywhere, with lasers for eyes!

Faster than trains and planes and cars,
Taller than rockets blasting to Mars.

Robots so beautiful like stars in the sky,
Amazing robots that backflip and fly!

The Robot Junk Yard is the place to be!
But one little robot said...

"What about me?"

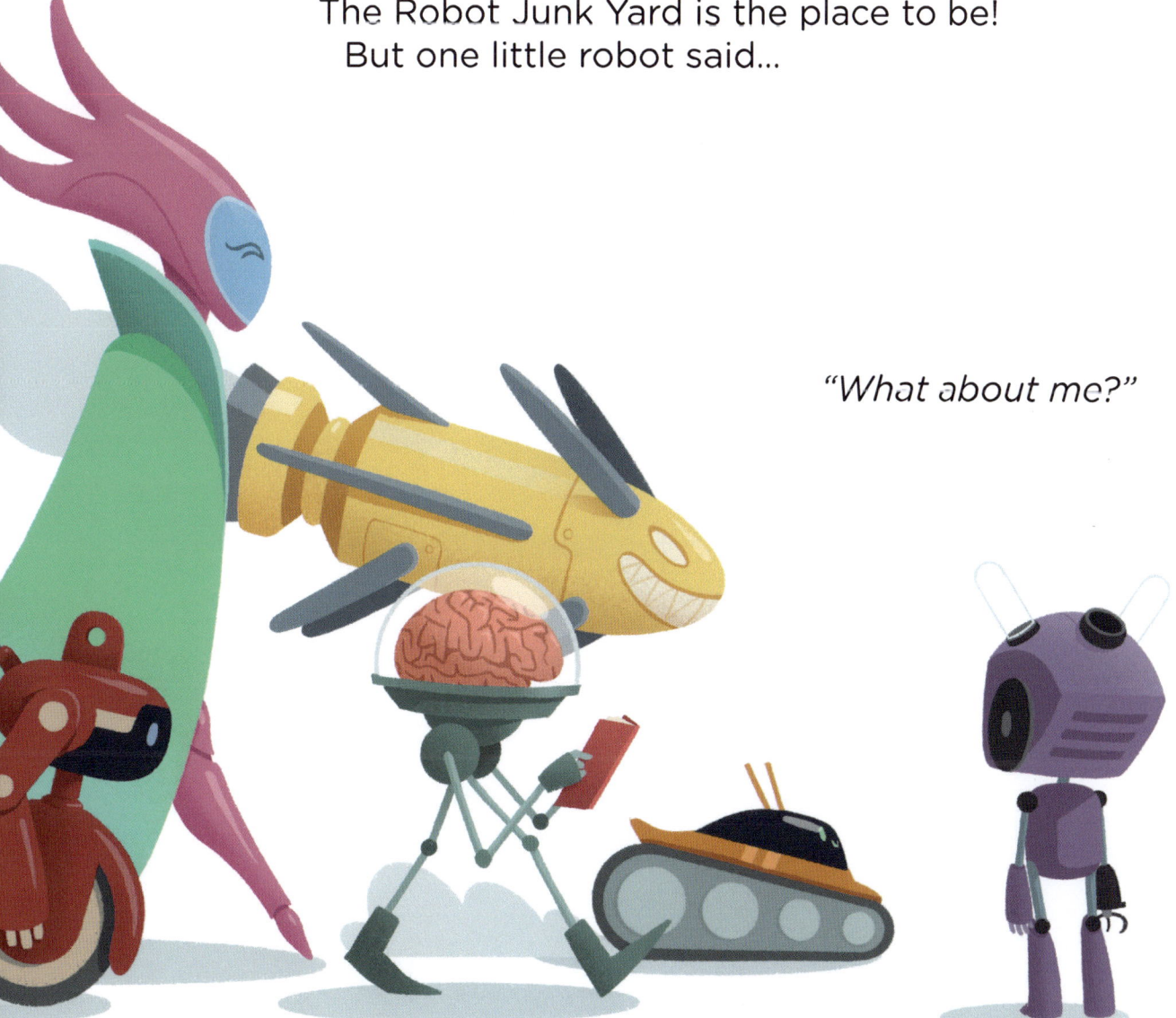

Glitch didn't feel talented, Glitch didn't feel cool,
Glitch wasn't the brightest robot in school.

They didn't have the newest or shiniest stuff,
They didn't feel tall, or big and tough.

Glitch didn't feel special, Glitch couldn't compare,
To all of the robots living in there.

But just before Glitch's battery went flat,
Their best friend Shift said, *"Don't get like that!"*

*"What's up with you? Are you ok?
You don't seem your happy self today!"*

"I'm done with being this boring machine,
I want to be the best robot that you've ever seen!"

They needed a plan and a change of gear.
Suddenly, Glitch had an idea!

"We'll go on an adventure, an amazing quest,
and find all the pieces to make me the best!"

The two little robots set off together,
This would be the GREATEST day ever!

*"I could be the fastest with lightning speed,
Come on, Shift, I know what I need."*

Glitch grabbed some wheels, a jet pack and tape,
and created a pair of turbo skates!

Glitch whizzed, zoomed, skidded and flew,
Shift alongside like best friends do.

"Go on, Glitch! You're the fastest, WOW!
Do you feel a bit more special now?"

"Not yet, Shift! I won't stop, NEVER!
I'm going to be the..."

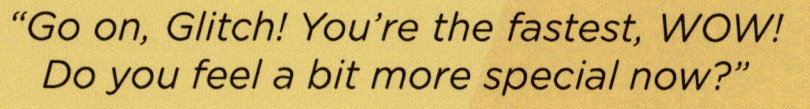

"TALLEST ROBOT EVER!"

With springs and bolts, ladders and pegs, Glitch built a pair of extendable legs.

Touching the clouds that floated so high, Reaching all the way up to the sky!

Wibbling and wobbling all over the town,
Shift waved at Glitch from down on the ground.

*"With extendable legs and turbo skates,
Surely now you must feel great?"*

*"Not yet, Shift! I won't stop, NEVER!
I'm going to be the..."*

"COOLEST ROBOT EVER!"

Glitch added anything that they could find,
Accessories, hairstyles, all one of a kind.

A pair of cool glasses, a phone and some bling,
A necklace and crown – they felt like a king!

A karaoke machine for singing out loud,
Some glittery outfits shining so proud.

Glitch used to hide and stay out of sight,
But now they were shining in their own spotlight!

Shift ran over, *"It's been so much fun!
Come on, Glitch, surely you're done?*

*If you add too much then what will you do?
If you aren't careful, you won't look like you."*

Glitch looked at Shift, a cheeky smile glowing,
Didn't Shift know they were just getting going?!

*"Not yet, Shift! I won't stop, NEVER!
I'm going to be the…"*

"STRONGEST ROBOT EVER!"

With steel and shields stuck together,
Glitch built their armour bigger than ever.

Padded arms and ginormous chest,
Becoming stronger than all the rest.

Weight lifting champion, Number One Pro,
Nothing too heavy to put on a show!

But Shift looked worried, Glitch was starting to shake,
"If you add any more... it could be a mistake!"

*"Stop worrying, Shift! I can't stop NEVER!
I'm going to be the..."*

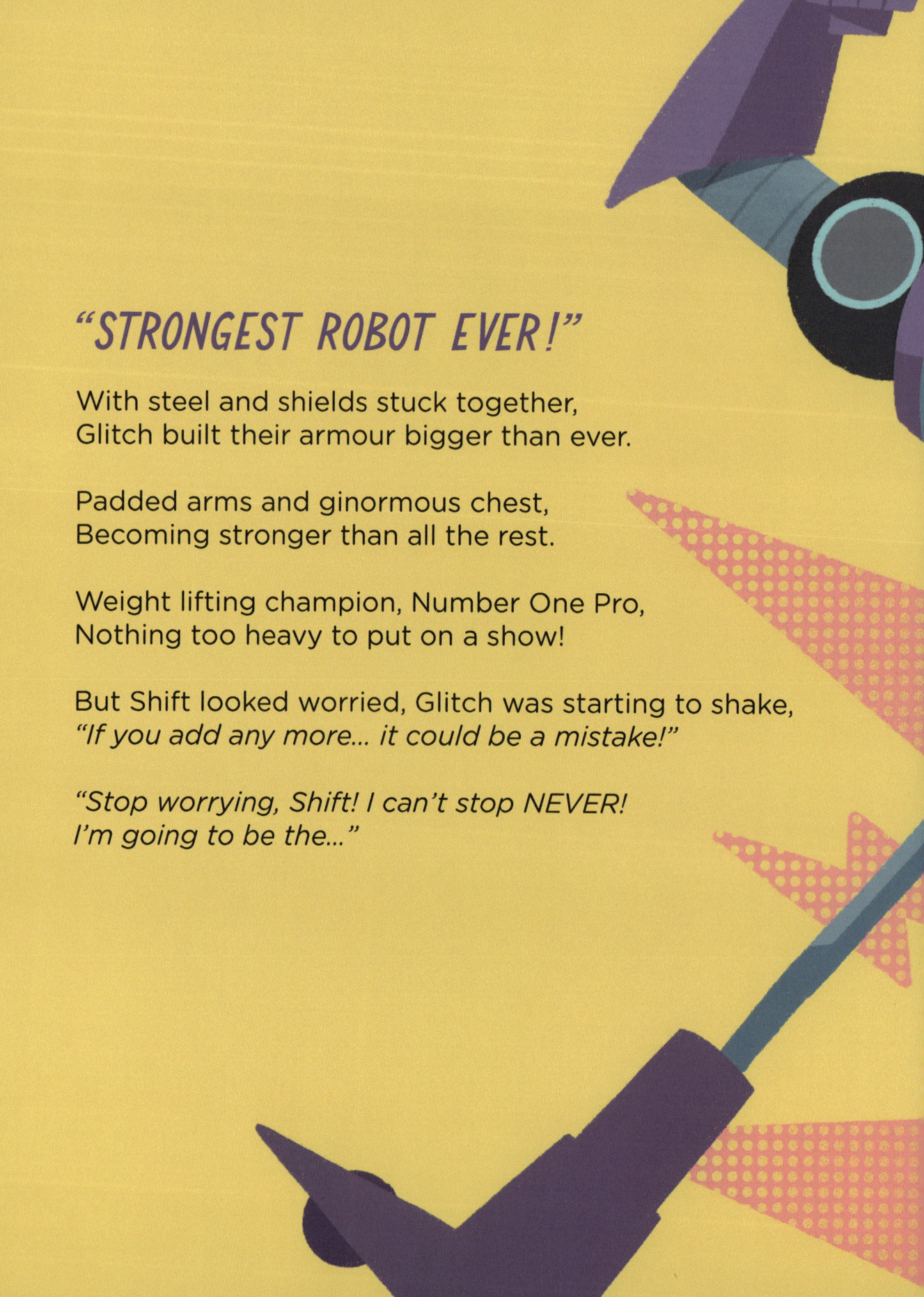

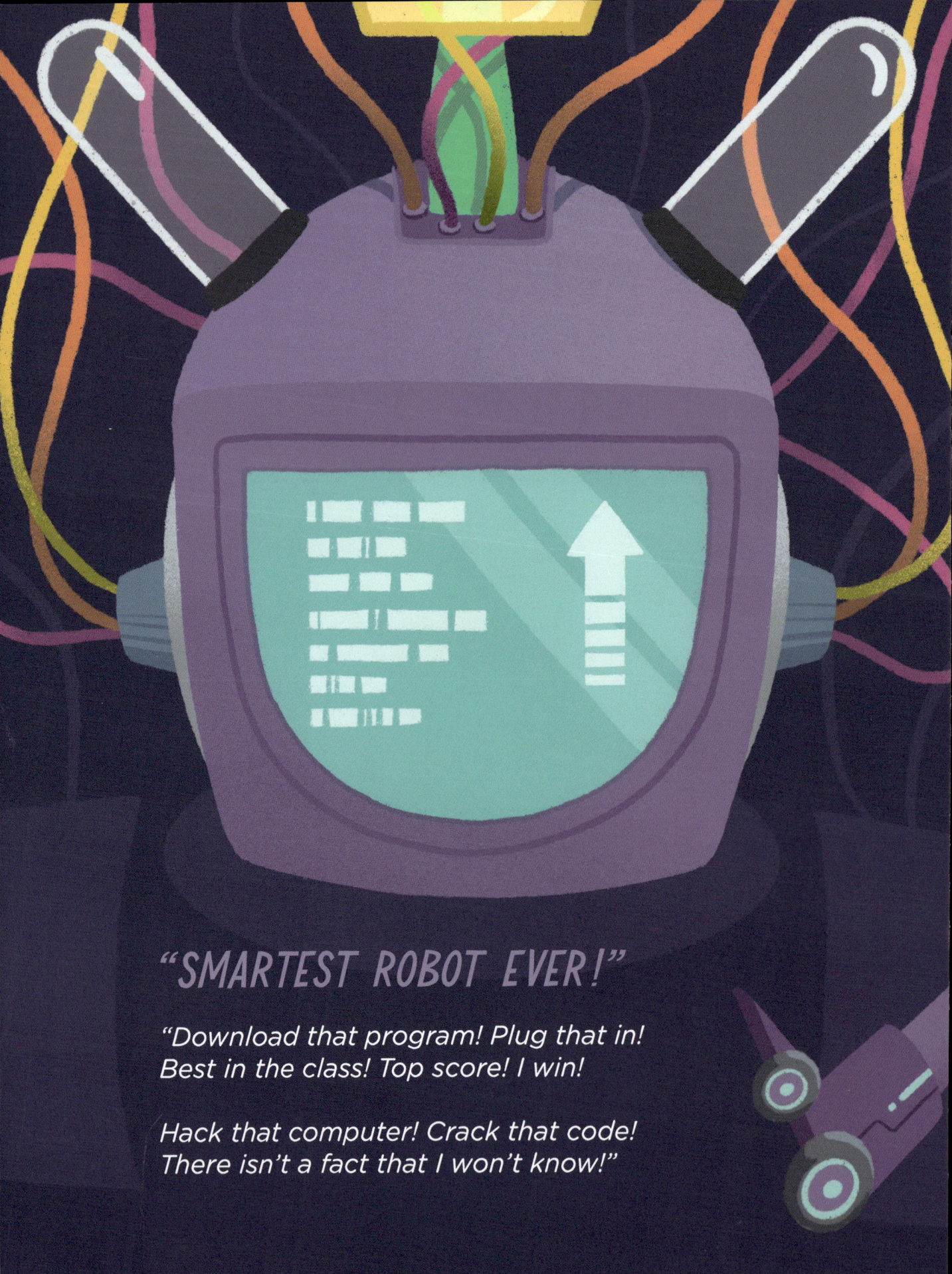

But then Shift heard a noise... a creak and a twitch,
"You're going to fall! Watch out, Glitch!"

It was all too much, Glitch staggered and stumbled,
Parts started falling, Glitch toppled and tumbled.

Shift took cover and hid in a dash,
Glitch shouted out *"I'm going to......"*

Glitch was in pieces all over the floor,
They couldn't get up or move anymore!

The things they'd gathered from the junkyard of fun,
Now seemed worthless, broken and done.

Being cool, fast, tall or strong
Wasn't what mattered all along...

Part by part, bit by bit,
The pieces of Glitch started to fit.

And just like that, with help from their friend,
Glitch the robot, was back on the mend.

*"Thank you, Shift, you're the best friend ever.
Without you, I wouldn't be back together!"*

*"I'll always be here, you know that's true,
But it's important to remember what makes you, you!*

*Don't forget, you are always enough,
Even when things get hard or tough.*

*You're kind, generous, brave and strong,
I could see it... all along.*

Don't ever think you're not enough, NEVER!"

Printed in Great Britain
by Amazon